FROM
FREAK-OUT
TO
F*CKING FINE

a journal for finding calm
when everything goes to sh*t

CAITLIN PETERSON

CASTLE POINT BOOKS
NEW YORK

www.castlepointbooks.com

The Castle Point Books trademark is owned by Castle Point Publications, LLC.
Castle Point books are published and distributed by St. Martin's Publishing Group.

ISBN 978-1-250-27382-6 (trade paperback)

Cover design by Katie Jennings Campbell
Interior design by Joanna Williams and Noora Cox

Images used under license from Shutterstock.com

Our books may be purchased in bulk for promotional, educational,
or business use. Please contact your local bookseller or the
Macmillan Corporate and Premium Sales Department at 1-800-221-7945,
extension 5442, or by email at MacmillanSpecialMarkets@macmillan.com.

First Edition: 2021

10 9 8 7 6 5 4 3 2 1

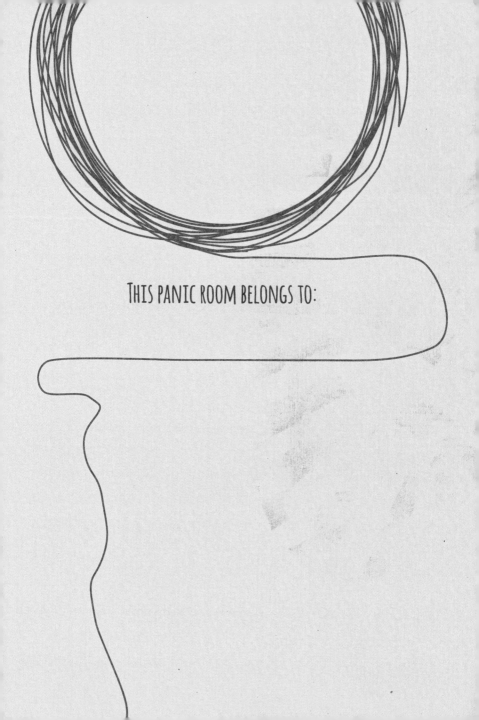

THIS PANIC ROOM BELONGS TO:

INTRODUCTION

For some of us, quietly repeating "breathe in, breathe out" while we sit cross-legged and envision dewy forests or peaceful ripples of water ratchets up our anxiety levels that much fucking higher. That's just how we're built. But when the shit hits the fan, we still need to find a way to stay cool. Enter *From Freak-Out to F*cking Fine*, a journal that understands your real life and how you're bent and gives you permission to productively flip out en route to a better place. How fun is that?

Each page is designed to help shepherd you through the valley of anxiety and back onto the road to happiness. With sweary prompts that help you process your feelings—and kick the fuckers to the curb if they don't serve you—this quirky journal is a relatable and perfect antidote to a rough day. So the next time someone tells you to "just breathe," don't throw a fucking chair; grab a pen and find your own path to fucking fine!

GO AHEAD, DR P THE FUCKING BALL

BEFORE THE CRASH

Even the Guinness World Records holder for most objects juggled (11) can only keep them all in the air for mere seconds and two catches each, then shit begins to crash to the ground. What are all the crazy balls you are attempting to juggle this week? Fill them in and then cross out at least one that you can honestly let drop or toss to someone else before you find yourself crashing.

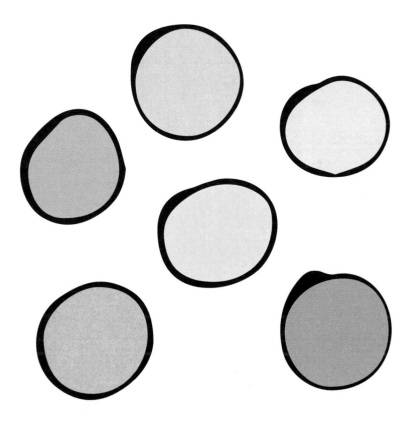

Own Your Body

Thinking happy, calming thoughts doesn't work for everyone. Another approach: invite that tension in for a glass of wine and sit with it. Really feel it in each part of your body, starting at your feet. Are your toes clenched? Fist tightened? Forehead stretched?

Then just when the bitch is getting a little too comfortable, release it all to the curb and tell it to fuck off. Wherever you felt the most tension, cover that area with a big, strong "FU!" above.

FLAWS AND ALL

To roughly quote Confucius, "Better a diamond with a fucking flaw than a pebble." Rather than panic every time less-than-shiny-and-happy traits emerge or lament that everyone else has their shit together, face and embrace your flaws with a big fucking hug.

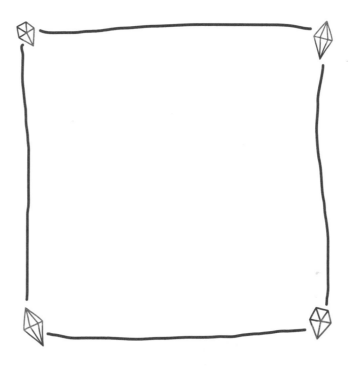

Draw your worst character trait to the extreme. Tend to be annoyingly late? Draw the person waiting for you aged 10 years. Then smile at how gloriously fucked up we all are together.

Into the Raging Waters

As you look out into the horizon of your coming week, what wave do you sense threatening your calm waters? Go ahead, splash and thrash like a mofo by venting here—but just for a minute.

_____

_____

_____

_____

_____

Now think of a few ways you can go straight at that giant like a fucking world champion surfer, rather than try to imagine it away or doggy-paddle furiously as fuck from it in a foam of panic. See yourself rising above it and riding in to peaceful shores on your own terms.

Let It All Out

Mellow Muzak is for waiting on hold. What you need is release.
Queue up the most emo song to which you know all the words. As
you scream or sob along with the lyrics, write in bold-as-fuck block
letters some of the words that resonate with how you're feeling.

Let your gut lead you to how to finish off this song session. Do you
want to go back and scratch out the words, or do you want to live
with them for a bit while you color them like a rainbow? Choose
whatever makes you feel happy as a fucking clam.

Damn that
SCENTED
CANDLE

CLEAR THE AIR

When we're feeling anxious as fuck, we may be tempted to find a calming quick fix. (Chamomile, anyone?) The result is often just stuffing the feelings under the bed or in the closet to bust their way back out later. Air out your anxious feelings here by covering this page with as many words as you can for how you're truly feeling. *Then* you can light that lavender candle and move the fuck on.

LAUNCH BREAK

Toss That Tension

Don't worry, no one is asking you to meditate in a quiet space. But focus on two things for just a minute: something you can launch (safely, *not* a chair) and a wide-open space. Possibilities: Drive golf balls in a field. Skip stones across water. Toss a tennis ball to your dog in the backyard. Even crumple up a piece of paper and throw it across the room. Imagine whatever is weighing on you inside the launching object, then go full fucking throttle on it. How did it feel?

Incoming rant...

Text Connections

Addiction recovery advocate Christopher Ferry so wisely sums up the best of friendships: "A friend is someone who listens to your bullshit, tells you that it is bullshit, and listens some more." Write down the names of a few people you can always call or text with your BS at any time of day or night to feel fucking better.

FREAKING
OUT HERE

NAME THE PANIC

When freaked-out emotions hit, they can feel like they're attached to you for life. But just like that freaky aunt or uncle, it can help to remember that you are only loosely related. Use the same strategy as with those strange relations—give your anxious feelings a silly name, whatever feels right to you. Separating them from everything else in your life takes away some of their control. In fact, you might find you have a whole family of fuckers in your head—from work anxiety to relationship anxiety. Name them fondly below.

Pace Under Pressure

Whether you're waiting for an important phone call or weighing a big decision, your body responds with the energy shot it thinks you need. So, don't fight the urge to fucking move: walk it off. Simply pacing around the room gives the adrenaline an outlet so it doesn't terrorize you—or turn you into an asshole who terrorizes everyone in your path. On the left side of the arrows below, write how you feel as you begin; on the right side, write how you want to feel. Focus on getting there.

CARPE

fucking

DIEM

Say Yes to Selfish

Call it fucking *self-care* if you need to. Whatever you call it, give yourself a day in the next two weeks to spend however you want—no explanations needed, whether you want to go hang gliding or just hang out with classic movies on Netflix until it asks if you're still alive. What's your pleasure? Plan it below, then make that shit happen.

HIGH-OCTANE

FRIEND

FUEL OR FIRE?

Sometimes, we worry more about shutting down our emotions than we may need to—and find ourselves in a whole damn pressure-filled cycle. If you asked the important people in your life about scenarios in which they are glad you don't hold back your surge of emotions, what would they say? Not sure? Ask them.

How can you keep your emotions fueling those relationships and not creating dangerous sparks?

Let that cookie

crumble

SMASH THE VISION

We've all been there, looking forward to biting into a perfect cookie. Or maybe your pleasure is a taco packed to the fucking shell. But then, the cookie or taco crumbles. Have your moment, then engage in a complete demolition. All the glorious ingredients are still there; grab a spoon or fork and dig in. Although your food is not your original vision of loveliness to behold, focus on...

HOW IT SMELLS

HOW IT TASTES

HOW FUCKING FUN IT WAS TO DESTROY

What's the crumbling situation in your life that may still have all the ingredients for something pretty damn good?

Meet My MONSTER

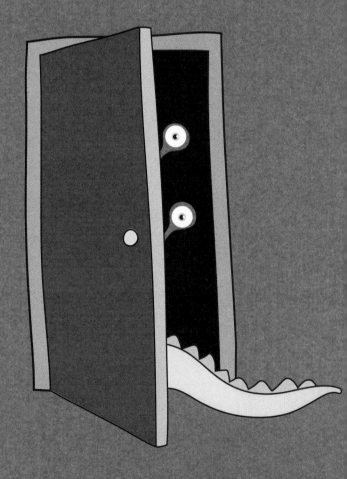

Scary Situations

Often, our anxious or angry feelings seem to have a life of their own. Draw a scary monster or villain that represents the worst of your freak-outs.

But every nemesis has a way to defeat it. (Have you learned *nothing* from horror films?) Remind yourself here what actions tamed some of your worst freak-out sessions, so you can pull out your list of weapons when you need it.

_____

_____

_____

STRESS BLOWS

BREATHE OUT THE BULLSHIT

Sure, you can get all sweet and blow bubbles into the air or blow the seeds off a dandelion as you imagine your fucking cares drifting away. But if you want to do something that actually triggers a reaction in your body, throw your hands (well, one hand) up in the air, right in front of your lips, and blow on your thumb as you make a thumbs up. The secret: Blowing on your thumb stimulates the vagus nerve, which tells your body to lower your blood pressure and decrease your heart rate. Other ways to stimulate the vagus nerve for calming benefits:

SING

Wash face with cold water

GARGLE

Massage feet

Hum

Circle the ideas you would be most likely to try.

BE BRUTALLY HONEST

We all fuck things up every day. Some we regret, some not so much. What recent fuckups do you wish you could take back?

_____

_____

_____

_____

_____

What situations, which seemed like fuckups at the time, are you actually glad happened because they forced something to come to light?

_____

_____

_____

_____

_____

_____

A Sweary Challenge

If mantras like "I am at peace" and "One with the world" are not quite your style, here is another approach. Come up with 20 sweary ways to say "calm." Let your creativity go wild, then put a star next to your favorite.

1. _____

2. _____

3. _____

4. _____

5. _____

6. _____

7. _____

8. _____

9. _____

10. _____

11. _____

12. _____

13. _____

14. _____

15. _____

16. _____

17. _____

18. _____

19. _____

20. _____

So fucking
HUMAN

WELCOME THE SPILL

Let's send a little message to that brain that can't seem to let go of the shit. Fill a glass of water to the brim and hold it away from your body. For a moment, it seems manageable. Try to do it for any length of time, and your arm screams "mercy!" Anxious feelings are the same way. We can only hold them for so long. What glass do you need to put down? Or can you let just a little water spill out to lighten the load?

_____

_____

_____

_____

_____

_____

_____

_____

_____

Social Standing

Whether you Snapped or felt Tik'ed off, think back to your worst freak-out on social media. What triggered you, and what person and response brought you the most support and comfort?

_____

_____

_____

_____

_____

_____

Is there someone you should consider unfollowing based on a response that only escalated the emotions for you?

_____

_____

_____

_____

_____

ACQUIRED TASTE

When your emotions run strong, it's not always a bad thing. It can also mean that you're fiercely loyal and live your life with passion. List the strong emotions that sometimes get you into trouble on the left below. Fill in the right side with ways your strong emotions benefit you and those around you. In the middle, insert emotions that could go either way.

LOSE THE LABELS

Cover this page with all the bullshit labels you've ever been called to your face, behind your back, or on social media. Maybe there are some shitty labels you give yourself when you're frustrated.

Now go back and cross them all out like you mean it. (The next page is expendable in case you rip through the paper in true freak-out style.) You can't stop the name calling completely, but you can let that shit go so it doesn't rule your world.

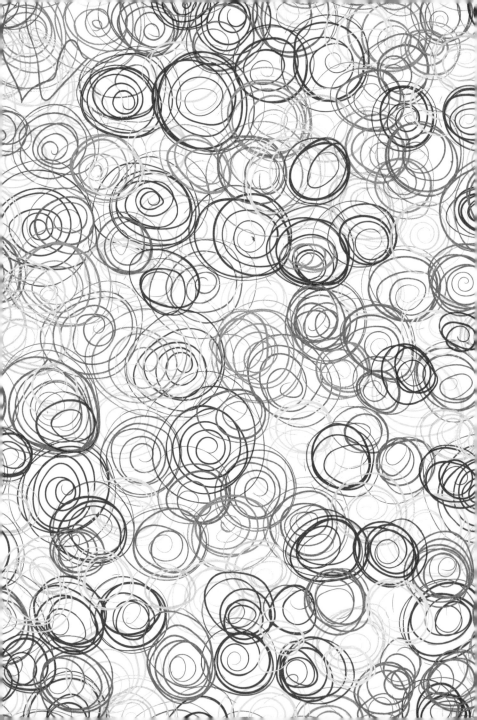

Stay Colorful

Full of hot air? Celebrate the energy you can channel by coloring in the message below.

STAND BACK

and watch my fucking liftoff

Tidy the
FUCK UP

TIME FOR A CLEAN START

If you're not feeling in a good headspace, look around your physical living space. What makes you feel sad, angry, or tense as fuck?

_____

_____

_____

_____

_____

_____

_____

_____

_____

_____

Box it up and stash it away if it's something you might need later. Send it out to the curb or donate it if it's time to part ways permanently.

Give
STRESS
the
FINGER

SMOOTH THE ROUGH SPOTS

Can't put your finger on what is bothering you? Well, actually, you can. Find a smooth stone to rub between your fingers. Even if meditation and "worry stones" are too woo-woo for you, the simple act of fidgeting with anything you can hold will refocus your twitchy mind. How do you feel...?

BEFORE:

_____

_____

_____

_____

_____

AFTER:

_____

_____

_____

_____

_____

Slam Some Doors

When frustration builds, sometimes slamming doors is totally necessary. You can do this literally (just warn any innocent bystanders first) to release some tension. But the better step is setting stronger fucking boundaries in your life. What doors do you need to close, or at least hang stricter rules on?

WHAT THE FUCCULENT

Dig In to Those Feelings

The next time you feel just plain fucking overwhelmed, find a place where you can really connect with some dirt—aside from social media. Maybe it's a backyard garden or a local park—or even that unopened bag of topsoil you bought with dreams of starting an herb garden. Spend some time digging like a kid on a mission to make mudpies, or kick off your shoes to let your feet feel the ground. Give yourself permission to get dirty. How does it feel?

_____

_____

_____

_____

_____

_____

_____

_____

_____

_____

HIT THE HILL

At any point in time, we're moving toward some higher peak and exhilarating liftoff in life. The climb to get there can be fucking torture. What height are you inching toward right now, and is there anything you can do to pick up speed?

_____

_____

_____

_____

_____

In what scenic attractions can you find calm along the way?

_____

_____

_____

_____

_____

No for an Answer

What *no*s have you heard in your life lately that have brought you down? Are there any that you could reasonably argue and turn around? Sort the *revisit*s from the *let go*s. Fire yourself up for one more take for the *revisit*s then move the fuck on—whatever the outcome.

_____ ☐ REVISIT ☐ LET GO

_____ ☐ REVISIT ☐ LET GO

_____ ☐ REVISIT ☐ LET GO

_____ ☐ REVISIT ☐ LET GO

_____ ☐ REVISIT ☐ LET GO

_____ ☐ REVISIT ☐ LET GO

_____ ☐ REVISIT ☐ LET GO

_____ ☐ REVISIT ☐ LET GO

TRUE CHARACTER

When we fuck up, we may instantly feel like the villain. But it's far from the end of the tale. Create a plot twist that transforms you into the fucking magnificent hero of the story. What character traits enable you to come to the rescue in some unexpected and outrageous way?

_____

_____

_____

_____

_____

_____

_____

_____

_____

_____

_____

GOOD SHIT on the HORIZON

BOOK IT NOW

On days when it feels like the apocalypse is just around the corner, we all need things to look forward to and remind us better times are just ahead. What are three things in the next few months you can ink in on your calendar now?

1. _____

   _____

   DATE: _____

2. _____

   _____

   DATE: _____

3. _____

   _____

   DATE: _____

Mark them big and bold and display the dates somewhere they look you straight in the eye each day as you count down.

CRYING TIME

Crying isn't a weakness. It makes you a badass who is totally comfortable with coming unhinged and showing some fucking authenticity. What is guaranteed to help you shed some tears and feel better afterward?

THIS SONG:

_____

THIS MOVIE OR SHOW:

_____

THIS MEMORY:

_____

SOMETHING ELSE:

_____

Just Dive In

When we're thinking about taking a risk, we drive our emotions into an all-out tizzy as we walk back and forth on the damn diving deck. By the time we approach the ladder, we feel too paralyzed or exhausted to take that first step. What leap of faith can you take this week to push yourself into a worthy new challenge even before your head has a chance to catch up?

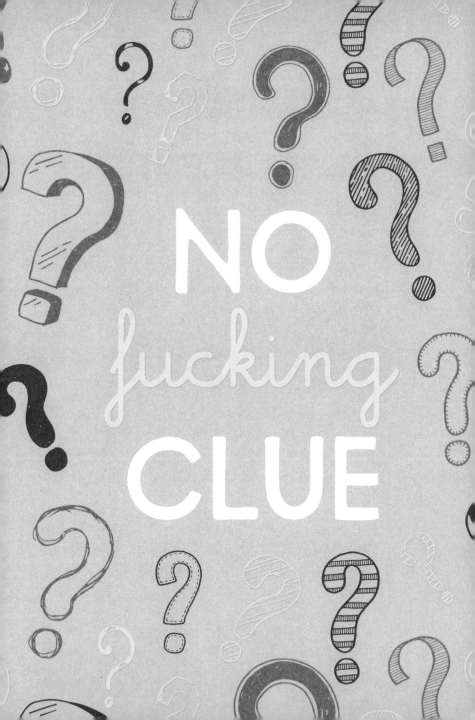

CLEAR YOUR HEAD

What unknowns in your life drive you fucking crazy? Next to each, make an intention to leave it a mystery or find a way to move toward an answer.

_____ LEAVE IT or SOLVE IT

_____ LEAVE IT or SOLVE IT

_____ LEAVE IT or SOLVE IT

_____ LEAVE IT or SOLVE IT

_____ LEAVE IT or SOLVE IT

_____ LEAVE IT or SOLVE IT

_____ LEAVE IT or SOLVE IT

_____ LEAVE IT or SOLVE IT

_____ LEAVE IT or SOLVE IT

SWEEP AWAY THE CRITICS

What physical or emotional area of your life gets constantly called out by others although you're satisfied with the state of affairs, no matter how messy? Write a breakup letter to your critics, and release the weight of judgments.

_____

_____

_____

_____

_____

_____

_____

_____

_____

_____

_____

_____

A Salute to Wild Streaks

No one can be calm 24/7—they're just really good actors. So, don't be so damn hard on yourself when you have freak-out moments. Emotions have ebbs and flows that are completely natural. Cover this page with as many examples of fucking beautiful wild streaks (from summer thunderstorms to beach hair) as you can.

Drop the Baggage

As you watch all those packed suitcases cycle around the conveyor belt in your head, do a quick inventory of the situations making you freak out right now.

_____

_____

_____

_____

_____

Now go back and cross out any shit you've gotten pulled into that isn't yours. What's your exit plan to pass that baggage off to its rightful owner?

_____

_____

_____

_____

_____

_____

HERE IS MY WHOLE FUCKING HEART

DROP THE SHIELD

It's not unusual to feel more freedom to show unguarded emotions around certain people. (You might, however, rein in the swearing around Nana.) But always holding back from someone can stifle the relationship. Is there someone you're protecting too much from your true emotions, and what do they need to hear from you?

Safe Spaces

You can't wait for a visit to a deserted island to let out everyday angst. Think about the places you spend the most time on typical days, then plan where in those settings you can go to find a fucking moment of freak-out without judgment or repercussions.

_____

_____

_____

_____

_____

_____

_____

_____

_____

_____

_____

_____

_____

Kitchen Therapy

Rough day? Head to the kitchen and pull out the cutting board. Choose a recipe that requires lots of chopping so you can get out all your frustrations. Ideas: chili, stir fry, salsa, or gumbo. Go for French onion soup if you want to go full-out release for ugly crying. Record the fucking cathartic experience here.

HOW IT FELT TO CHOP:

_____

_____

_____

HOW THE RECIPE TURNED OUT:

_____

_____

_____

_____

_____

No Holding Back

The weight of unspoken words can be freakishly heavy. What did you want to say to someone so fucking badly today but knew it wouldn't really be productive? Release everything here and now—no matter how messy.

_____

_____

_____

_____

_____

_____

_____

_____

_____

_____

_____

_____

Hear Me
ROAR
& Purr

MOOD ANIMALS

Moods can make you seem like a lion or a kitten. Yet, each reaction is still completely you. Come up with an animal that represents your most anxious or angry mood. Then envision what animal most captures your chill-as-fuck side. Draw both animals hanging out together in crazy harmony below.

FREAK OUT, MOVE ON

Emotions can be damming and damning, keeping you from going for a goal you really want. What have you always wanted to do that your emotions are holding you back from?

THE GOAL:

_____

_____

THE EMOTIONS:

_____

_____

WORST-CASE SCENARIO:

_____

_____

HOW CAN YOU GET OUT OF YOUR OWN FUCKING WAY AND MAKE SOMETHING HAPPEN?

_____

_____

SO NOT HELPING

When you're having a fucking moment, what ways do others try to help that only provoke your emotions?

Who needs to hear that they're only fueling the fire?

TURN IT UP

There may be a time and a place for the sounds of gentle water and chimes. But sometimes we need stronger help drowning out all the internal dialogue. List 10 loud sounds that are oddly comforting to you.

1. _____

2. _____

3. _____

4. _____

5. _____

6. _____

7. _____

8. _____

9. _____

10. _____

COME
undone

You're Worth the Wait

Take a stab at what you think your freakishly full to-do list should look like for tomorrow.

○ _____

○ _____

○ _____

○ _____

○ _____

○ _____

○ _____

○ _____

There are times when you just need to leave shit undone in order to throw yourself a life preserver. Go back and cut out a few things that honestly aren't essential. Replace them with ways to grab a few fucking moments of calm in your day.

FUCK,
THAT'S GOOD!

INSTANT COMFORT

From your favorite dessert to a blanket that lays on weight but somehow magically takes weight away, what little indulgences can easily take you from WTF to relief in mere minutes? Create the elements of your oasis in words or pictures below.

Know Your Indicators

Dogs and cats often run and hide when bad weather is approaching. What signs can help you sense that you're about to lose your shit?

Are there ways you can take shelter and minimize collateral damage until the front passes?

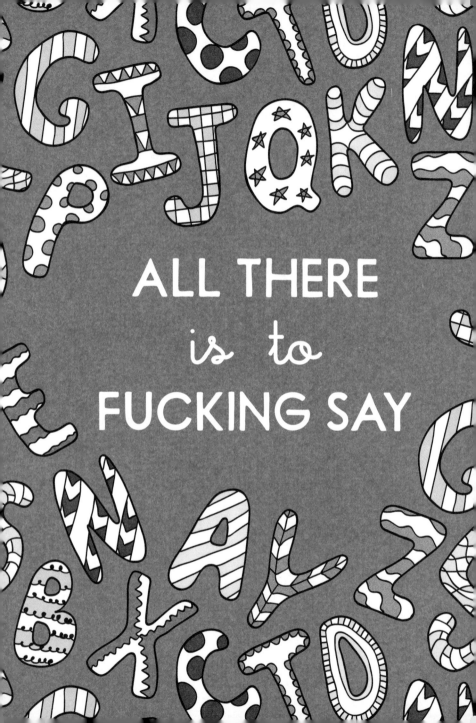

DICTIONARY OF DE-ESCALATION

Think about how the word *moist* can conjure up such strong emotions in certain people. Make a list of words that are so fucking silly or absurd that they can de-escalate whatever else is running through your mind. (*Kerfuffle,* anyone?) When you feel a freak-out coming on, think of your words in your mind or physically write them on a piece of paper.

_____   _____

_____   _____

_____   _____

_____   _____

_____   _____

_____   _____

_____   _____

MAKE SOME SPACE

Idolizing the past can put a lot of pressure on the present to live up to hazy memories. What pictures of the past are you holding on to with a vise grip? Draw them here in pencil.

Now go back and erase the pictures you need to release. Leave the squares blank in order to make way for fucking beautiful things still ahead.

DECISIONS, DECISIONS

Think back to times in your life when your emotions led you to make a decision. Describe one decision that turned out to be for the best and the emotions behind it.

_____

_____

_____

_____

_____

Describe another decision that turned into a shitstorm and the emotions behind it.

_____

_____

_____

_____

_____

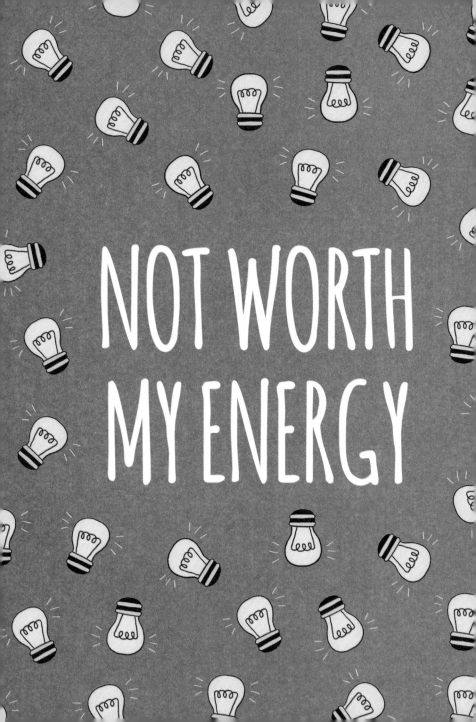

Transfer of Power

People and situations can suck energy from you like those old incandescent lightbulbs. Your electric bill deserves LED and so does your fucking life. In what areas can you walk away from the energy drains and transfer your energy to endeavors that brighten your days?

ENERGY DRAIN   ››› *transfer to* ›››   BRIGHTER DAYS

MOMENTS OF FUCKING FINE

Days can be swayed by the craziest few minutes that have a way of pushing everything else over the edge. Make a list of all the moments you said "fuck this!" aloud or in your head today. Then see if you can make an even longer list of things that you found fucking brilliant—or at least bearable.

FULL STOP

Starting Signals

Bad days often start with anxious thoughts. What emotional derailments are known to threaten your head first thing in the morning?

_____

_____

_____

_____

_____

What little morning routines could keep you tracking the fuck along a better route?

_____

_____

_____

_____

STEP AWAY

from the control button

Free Your Inner Control Freak

Knowing what you want and grabbing on to life can bring you success. But when you try to hold tight to what you don't truly have control over, you're likely to wind up frustrated as fuck. What are the things you keep trying to micromanage the shit out of, but aren't actually in your power to change?

In what area(s) of your life can you focus your control for real positive action?

DEEP FEELINGS

We often get into the biggest emotional conflicts with the people we care most about. What emotions collide with the people you love the most?

_____

_____

_____

_____

How can you help them navigate through your freak-out and not take it personally?

_____

_____

_____

_____

_____

love you

THIS WAY TO CALM

People may freak out—and drive you to freak out with their response—when you take a different path, but you own your choices. Don't waste your damn time and sanity arguing the merits of your perspective over and over again. Celebrate your unique take on every fucking day by listing unpopular choices you're proud of below.

Hey,
sweary sister

MEET ME IN THE FREAK-OUT

Think about the one person in your life who truly gets you and will come to your rescue anytime, anyplace. Draw or post a picture of the two of you together below. What does this person say or do to either talk you down or make a ranting session even more fun?

FULL SPEED
AHEAD

Go for It

When your emotions are in overdrive, where can you transfer some energy? List five activities you can throw yourself into and enjoy some speed.

1. _____

2. _____ **20 50 70**

3. _____

4. _____

5. _____

Cleanse Your Feeds

What you focus on expands. It may be time to make some bad influences on your mood go *poof*. What accounts or contacts stir your emotions in a negative way? Commit to saying goodbye on social.

BUH-BYE

NOT TODAY

OVER THIS SHIT

Just for freeing fun, play a goodbye-themed song as you hit all the right "unfollow" buttons.

MEET MY MOODS

Isn't a little fucking emotional better than boring? List 10 things that are weird as fuck but wonderful about you.

1. _____

2. _____

3. _____

4. _____

5. _____

6. _____

7. _____

8. _____

9. _____

10. _____

END THE CHASE

It's easy to freak out when we see everyone else's perfectly curated lives on our screens. But they're never the whole picture. Prioritize passion over perfection, and you just might discover peace of mind. Find a photo of yourself in which you look far from perfect, but you're filled with fabulous energy. Post it below as a reminder of what's truly fucking fine and worthy of your focus.